A Guide to Orchids

Written by Stephen J Broderick

A simple guide to the fascinating subject of Orchids and their maintenance.

The booklet, although primarily aimed at the novice may also prove a valuable reference for the expert.

D1312850

Photographs: D Entwisle, Laura Broderick & www.bigphotostcock.com
Additional research: Rebecca Broderick
First edition 2006

Stephen J Broderick

Having studied and graduated from the University College of North Wales Bangor with a degree in Agriculture in 1984. Stephen then moved to work in the related area of Horticulture.

He has spent many years working for "Plants for Pleasure", a leading wholesaler of bonsai trees and related sundries to the Garden Centre trade.

In recent years he has developed a particular interest in orchids.

Aware of the mystique and general trepidation in which these plants are often seen. His set out to write this booklet in an easy to read and understand manner. The principal aim being to let the reader achieve maximum enjoyment from their orchid.

The booklet does not aim to be a definitive document on the subject, but rather a gentle introduction and useful reference tool.

Contents

Introduction

Of all the 'houseplants' available in Garden Centres today, perhaps the most popular and 'cool' to own is the Orchid

So what is so special about these plants?

Firstly it is the enormous diversity.

The family Orchidaceae is just about the largest flowering plant family. To date, approximately 30,000 wild species have been identified.

In addition many specially bred hybrids have been developed.

In the wild orchids range in size from plants one inch high with extremely small flowers to rambling vines of fifty feet in length with gigantic flowers of one foot across!

Orchids occur right across the globe from rain forests to mountain meadows, wetlands to semi arid regions, and from sea level to 14,000 feet.

The only exceptions are totally arid deserts and the polar areas.

In the wild most tropical and subtropical orchids grow on the trunks and branches of trees.

This explains why the growing medium supplied with Garden Centre bought orchids is high in woody fibrous content. This is often coconut bark and chips.

Orchids can make ideal houseplants if the correct species is chosen, as they do not require high levels or over zealous watering.

The sheer elegance and beauty of the orchid combined with its aura of sophistication help to explain their appeal.

Cattleya

History of Orchids

Orchids can be dated back as far as 15 million years by use of fossil records. This may seem old to you and I, but in botanical terms orchids are a mere youngster. Other plant families can be traced as far back as 100 million years!

This relative juvenility means that orchids are probably still undergoing the evolutionary process.

As a result of this, individual orchid genera can be quite easily crossed with each other resulting in hybrid genera.

Mankind has been captivated by the beauty and variety of orchids for many centuries.

As long ago as the fifth century b.c. Confucius compared the pleasure of seeing a group of friends to entering a room full of fragrant orchids.

The Chinese called these flowers "Lan".

Later, the name they were to become known by in the west was given to them (according to legend) by Theophrastus.
A student of Plato, he noted that the round bulbs of a common variety of European orchid were not dissimilar to male genitalia. Hence he gave it the name Orchis, from the Greek word for testicle!

As a consequence the Greeks believed they were a symbol of virility, and were even one of the main ingredients in love potions.

Eventually the name orchis became synonymous with the entire family and not just one genus (even though the majority of orchids do not have this type of root).

In the middle ages orchids played a role in herbal remedies. Aphrodisiacal powers were attributed to them.

Potions made from younger tubers were believed to lead to the conception of boys, while those made from older less firm tubers would result in female children.

It was thought that when dreamt about they represented the need to keep romance in a relationship.

By the beginning of the eighteenth century orchid collecting was becoming established in various parts of the world.

The well known spice plant and orchid (*Vanilla planifolia*) was introduced to British gardens in 1739. This further increased the popularity of orchids.

In the nineteenth century, orchids were in great demand. Plant auctions in London and Liverpool attracted wealthy buyers, who would regularly pay £500 for a single plant. Especially desirable plants would attract higher prices still.

The aristocratic growers of the nineteenth century were highly competitive and unlikely to divulge their cultural secrets to fellow collectors.

Of these early collectors, William Catley of Barnet is probably the most of famous. The popular Cattleya orchid is named after him.

This "orchid fever" inevitably had a down side.

This manifested itself in the systematic stripping of orchids from many forests.

Today orchid breeding is big business.

Nearly all orchids found on sale in UK Garden Centres will have been imported from highly specialised Dutch growers.

Orchid Anatomy

The vast majority of orchids have three distinguishing features, which when combined make them unique among flowering plants.

(i)   Three sepals
(ii)   Three petals
(iii)   A column

The **sepals** may look like petals but are in fact the remains of the flower bud.
The central uppermost is known as the dorsal sepal, whilst the lower two opposite each other are the lateral sepals.

The size of sepals can vary but they always located on the outer area of the flower with the petals within. The three sepals protect the flower when in bud.

In most other plants the sepals often remain green, however in orchids the sepals change from green to various colours when the bud is ready to open.

Like the sepals, orchids have three **petals.** These make up the inner parts of the blossom. Two of the petals are normal, however the third forms a special structure that is called a lip or labellum. In the wild this lip serves as a landing platform for the plants pollinator.

The lip is often differently coloured and may be highly decorated in order to attract specific insects.

The overall shape of orchid flowers is typically bilaterally symmetrical, (the left and right halves are mirror images of each other).

This is a necessity for effective pollination by bees.

Other natural pollinators of orchids are butterflies, gnats, flies, humming birds and even the occasional bat!

Anatomy of Orchid Flower

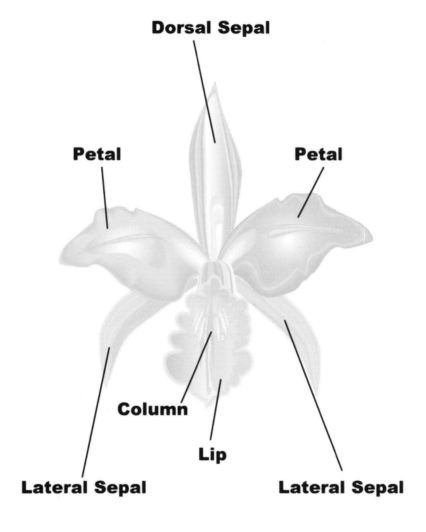

Dorsal Sepal

Petal

Petal

Column

Lip

Lateral Sepal

Lateral Sepal

Yet another unique characteristic of the orchid is the combination of the plants male and female reproductive organs.

These are fused together into a fleshy **column** or *gynostemium*.

The column is located inside the petals and can often be concealed by them.

At the top of the column are the male structures including the anthers. These produce pollen grains, which are often grouped together and are known as *pollina*.

Immediately below the anthers, but separated from them by a thin membrane is he female part of the orchid. This is called the *stigma.*

This consists of a sticky surface on which pollen must be placed upon in order to facilitate fertilisation.

This separation of the male and female parts means that self pollination is not possible.

The orchid therefore relies upon third party pollinators, as mentioned previously.

In practice most orchids are cross-pollinated.

A packet of pollen will attach to a particular place on the body of an insect and then be deposited on the stigma of the next flower it visits.

The need for insects etc. to pollinate, explains all the attention seeking colours, shapes and scents of orchids. The exact mechanism of pollination can very elaborate and many orchid species can only achieve this successfully with the help of a particular insect species.

Pollination produces a series of changes in the orchid.

Shortly after the flower will start to wilt. Pollen tubes grow towards the ovary.

When the ovules are fertilised, the seed capsule begins to enlarge and mature.

Each fully mature seed is very small, typically 1mm in diameter.
Such a small seed has a very small food reservoir and consequently its chances of success are limited.

The orchid balances this disadvantage with the production of vast amounts of seed.

A seed which germinates successfully emerges as a minute structure which resembles an underground stem. The new seedling can remain in this state for as much as two years.

Before further growth can take place the seedling must be infected by one of several species of fungi. The fungus will concentrate in the roots. These fungi are known as *mycorrhiza* (a derivation from the Greek for fungi and roots.)

A symbiotic relationship develops between the fungi and the plant. This means that they are both dependent upon each other for substances they cannot form themselves.

All being well the orchid will continue to grow and eventually flower.

In their natural habitat this whole process can take up to ten years, but can be as short as twenty months.

Two other important parts of the orchid worth mentioning are the roots and the leaves.

The **roots** of orchids vary according to the type of plant. The roots of *terrestrial* orchids (see page 12) branch out from the base of the plant. They often have a downy covering of hair and have a green tip which is actually the part that grows.

The *epiphytic* orchids (see below) often have aerial roots. These develop because of the environment in which these plants live.

As the plants live on the branches of trees they are unable to absorb water from the soil. Water is taken up from rainfall by these aerial roots and stored within them.

These roots also function as anchors for the plant, firmly attaching the orchid to the tree branch.

Another distinguishing feature of the orchid is that each root grows for only one year. It does not die after this time but it will not put on any further growth.

Orchid **leaves** perform the same functions as those of other plants. This mainly being to photosynthesise, (the

conversion of light into food).

The physical appearance of the leaves vary and is mostly governed by the habitat the plant occupies in the wild.

Although often arranged in rows opposite each other some orchids have only one main leaf, with the others being underdeveloped.

Orchids are divided into two main groups:

- Epiphytic orchids
- Terrestrial orchids

Epiphytic types live on the branches of trees and other plants. They are not to be mistaken with parasitic plants, as they do not derive food from the host plant.
Terrestrial orchids live on the ground. Initially all orchids were of this type, poor light and other plant competition forced some up into the branch canopy.

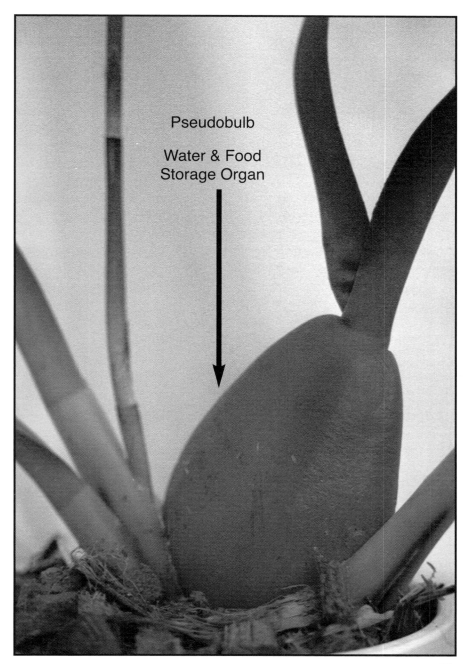

Pseudobulb

Water & Food
Storage Organ

Choosing an Orchid

In order to ensure a good chance of success with your orchid here a few points to look out for when buying.

- Firstly take into consideration where about at home you intend to keep your plant. Some varieties thrive in low light levels others prefer a brighter location.

- Make sure the orchid is labelled with its full name. If not you will be unable to find out the correct care and conditions required.

- Check the soil or growing medium, this should not be too wet. Rotting roots can soon result in the demise of the whole plant!

- Pay attention to the overall appearance of the plant. Make sure the plant shows no visible signs of pest damage or infection. Do not buy a plant with wilting, damaged or leaves which have lost their sheen.

- Steer clear of plants that have been kept in a draughty location, such as by the door in a Garden Centre. This is particularly important when buying during the winter months

- Do not buy a plant just because they are being sold off cheaply. There will be a reason for this. Such a purchase is invariably a false economy.

Care Conditions

The following are the major factors that need to be considered and controlled when looking after an orchid (or any other plant for that matter).

- Temperature
- Watering/Humidity
- Light levels

Temperature

The ideal temperature required for your orchid will be dependent upon the particular type you have bought.

Many orchids do like fresh air. However as rule of thumb avoid extremes of cold and heat and protect from cold draughts.

More specific temperature requirements for particular orchid types are given later in his booklet.

Watering & Humidity

Without doubt the most important factor to consider is watering. In the wild orchids do not live in moisture rich environments. Many orchids kept as houseplants are killed by over watering! Too much water can starve the roots of oxygen.

Epiphytic orchids should only be watered when the growing medium is very dry.

Terrestrial orchids require more water than their epiphytic cousins, the soil should never be allowed to dry out but neither should it become drenched.

When watering, it is good practice to use water at room temperature. To achieve this fill a small watering can and leave it to stand in the room for few hours. Allowing tap water to stand like this also has the additional benefit of allowing some of the chemicals therein to disperse.

Orchids prefer soft to hard water. Water hardness can be checked with your local water provider. If it is excessively hard, it may be worth considering softening it. This can be done either physically or chemically. An easier option may be to use freshly collected clean rainwater.

Although not native to wet environments many orchids do live in humid areas in the wild. This particularly applies to the epiphytic types.

Humidity levels can be increased in a number of ways. Perhaps the simplest is to sit your plant on shallow tray covered with horticultural grit and containing water.

The evaporating water from this "humidity tray" will increase the moisture content of the air around the plant, so mimicking conditions found in its natural habitat.

Small hand held misters are also of great use. Again make sure that the water inside the mister has been allowed to reach room temperature before using.
Mist regularly but avoid misting the flowers of the plant. Concentrate on the leaves only.

Light Levels

Light is vital for any plants survival as it is required for photosynthesis to take place.
Many orchids are native to densely forested environments.
Consequently they have adapted themselves to be able to survive in relatively low light levels.

This is particularly true for the ever popular 'Moth orchid' (*Phalaenopsis sp.*), making them an ideal houseplant.

Growing Mediums

As previously mentioned orchids have different root systems to those of most other houseplants. Due to their mainly epiphytic nature, they have thick and fleshy roots.

This type of root whilst having its advantages also has the major disadvantage of being very susceptible to rot if the plant is potted in a water holding compost.

Consequently orchids are normally grown in substrates which are very open and free draining.
The purpose of these mediums is to mimic the conditions in which the plants grow in the wild.

Orchid 'composts' will often be found to contain pieces of bark, perlite and charcoal.

A relative newcomer that is being increasingly used is rockwool, unlike bark, this has the advantage of not breaking down over time.

Other media that may be used include:-

- Lava rock
- Sphagnum Moss
- Clay pellets

Most orchid 'experts' have their own favourite recommendation.

Whatever is chosen must have a high air to water ratio.

Composts can be bought ready mixed from most good garden centres, alternatively make up own individual recipe!

A good basic mix would be 50% bark (Douglas fir bark is most commonly used), combined with 50% perlite (processed granules of volcanic rock).

Perlite is readily available and comes in different grades. Choose a coarse grade when mixing your own orchid compost.

Pots and containers

Historically orchids were often planted into clay pots. These pots provide the benefit of being heavy and therefore offer stability.

This can be particularly useful when potting larger orchids such as some of the *Dendrobiums,* which can have thick stems and large pseudobulbs.

In modern times plastic pots have prevailed over clay ones.

Good quality plastic pots are easily cleaned and do not retain cold or salts.

Many garden centres sell ceramic pot covers in which the orchid in a plastic pot can be placed.

Epiphytic orchids with aerial roots are often supplied in transparent plastic pots.

These pots allow light to the roots which enables photosynthesis, as would occur in the wild.

An added bonus of using transparent pots is the ability to monitor root growth and health.

Other containers include wooden baskets. Again these are useful for epiphytes as they allow plenty of light to the roots.

Indoors a plant in a wooden basket will dry out more quickly than one in a plastic pot, this should be taking into mind before buying or repotting.

A more specialist way of display is to grow an epiphyte on a slab of bark.
The plant must be firmly secured to the bark by natural fibres.

This method calls for high humidity, daily misting would be required. Adding a small amount of sphagnum moss to the planting will aid moisture retention.

Repotting

Repotting of orchids is generally done for two main reasons.

Either the orchid has

(i) Outgrown its pot
or
(ii) The growing medium has broken down. This will result in a less free draining compost which may become sodden.

If the latter is the case, it is important that repotting is done as soon as practically possible.
It is not advisable to repot orchids 'just for the sake of it'.
If possible repot when the plant is showing signs of putting on new growth at the shoots and roots.

To start, carefully ease the orchid out of its existing container. Remove all or as much as possible of the old growing medium. When doing this, take care not to damage the roots.

If any of the existing roots are dead or rotting, remove them using a clean sharp knife. This is also a good time to cut off any damaged or dying leaves and flowers.

Unless the plant is being heavily divided, or the plant is very overgrown use a pot one size larger than previously.

Moisten the new compost before repotting and add a layer to the bottom of the pot before inserting the orchid. Pack the medium firmly around the plants roots whilst keeping the shoots above the compost.

Any old growth should be placed against the side of the pot to allow plenty space for new shoots to develop. Use a stake if required.

Place in a shady position.

Do not water for approx. two weeks but do mist daily.

(i)

Remove the orchid from its existing pot, taking particular care not to damage the roots.

(ii)

Remove old growing medium and cut out any dead or rotting roots with a sharp knife or scissors.

(iii)

Place the orchid in moistened fresh compost, firmly packing the medium around the roots.

Orchid Genera

Cattleya

These orchids are named after William Cattley who is credited with blooming the first Cattleya orchid in Europe in 1818.

Cattleya orchids are typified by their large spectacular flowers. These flowers are often of various shades of lilac. Although white, cream and yellow flowers can be found within the genus.

In the USA cattleya orchids are commonly called "corsage orchids" as their blooms are often used in corsages because of their beauty and scent.

The genera also have large pseudobulbs and grow sympodially (all new shoots grow from these pseudo bulbs).

In the wild they are either epiphytic or lithophytic (grow on rocks).

Cattleya orchids are slow growing and usually only flower after they are five years old. They also have a relatively short flowering period when compared to other species.

They prefer semi shade or low light conditions. Unlike many houseplants they benefit from good air circulation around them. This is because in the wild they grow quite high up in the tree canopy.
They are best kept in a temperature between 12° - 30°C (55° - 86°F).

They can be allowed to dry out slightly between watering. Misting should be carried out regularly during the summer but is less important during the winter months.

A period of dormancy is necessary in order to flower.

Cattleya orchids can be prone to mealy bug. Check before buying!

Cymbidium

Cymbidiums are the oldest cultivated orchids, and were evidently grown in China 2,500 years ago.

The majority are epiphytic with just a few being terrestrial.

This genus can be generally characterised by their flowers which resemble glamorous daffodils.

The lip (lower sepal) is often ornately speckled. The leaves of the plant are numerous and again similar in appearance and growth habit to daffodils.

The flowers are quite large and can last for two to three months. Historically cymbidiums were often grown for use as cut flowers.

Cymbidiums prefer to be grown in quite cool conditions and can tolerate temperatures of just a few degrees.

Consequently they do not make ideal houseplants. Ideally they should be kept outside during the summer as they prefer warm days and cool nights if flowering is going occur

If placed outside they should be put in the shade or an area receiving some dappled sunlight.

The maximum summer temperature should be around 30°C (86°F) during the day.

During the following three seasons the night time temperatures should not exceed 13°C (55°F), but not drop below 8°C (46°F).

Cymbidiums should never be allowed to dry out and the compost should be kept moist.

Be vigilant for attacks by scale insects and spider mites.

Dendrobium

Dendrobiums

Dendrobiums make up a large genus consisting of approx. 1,600 species.

Having said this only a relative few are available commercially.

There are two major groups of dendrobium hybrids each having different requirements.

(i) *D. nobile*

These tend to have thick stems and are often referred to as bamboo orchids.

These hybrids make ideal greenhouse plants as they require plenty of light and can survive in temperature down to 8°C in the winter months.

(ii) *D..phalaenopsis*

As the name suggests the flowers are similar to those of the moth orchid (*phalaenopsis sp.*). They make good houseplants requiring slightly warmer conditions.

The flowering stems of both groups of dendrobiums are mostly multi flowered. These flowers are occasionally lusciously scented.

Both groups require little watering when in their dormant season. However when growing, regular watering is needed combined with frequent misting.

A good tip when buying dendrobium phalaenopsis is to pick one that is in flower rather than in bud. The reason for this is that they can react badly to change of position, and the buds may drop or never develop

Also remove any cellophane sleeving immediately as this can encourage botrytis.

Pests are not a particular problem with this genus.

Miltonia (Miltonopsis)

More commonly known as the 'Pansy Orchid', these plants produce trusses of flowers which are strikingly similar to the blotched flowers of winter pansies.

They are ideally suited to life as a 'houseplant' in that they are tolerant of and indeed thrive on warmth.

They also prefer shade and will respond poorly to being placed in a too well lit position. This will be indicated by the development of red or slightly yellow leaves

The attractive flowers will last for six to eight weeks in ideal conditions.

Particular care must be taken when watering Miltonia. They have fine sensitive roots which can be easily damaged by over or under watering. The compost must be free draining to avoid water logging, but must be kept slightly moist to avoid drying out.

If the plant dries out or the compost becomes too wet, growth is temporarily stopped. If this happens repeatedly a phenomena known as the 'concertina effect' can occur resulting in a series of folds in the leaves and shoots.

If the problem is over watering repot into fresh compost.

Miltonia are susceptible to attack by red spider mite and scale insects. As with other genera scale insects often locate in the base of the pseudobulbs.

Air circulation and misting will help prevent the damaging pest, red spider mite.

Regular misting during the summer will also keep their numbers down.

Soap based or biological controls are best used.

Paphiopedilum

Plants of this classic genus are commonly referred to as 'Slipper Orchids'. They are characterised by having a distinctive flower shape with a pitcher that resembles a slipper.

Before most homes had central heating, (which led to *phalaenopsis* becoming the best selling orchid), the 'Slipper Orchids' were the best known orchid 'houseplant'.

The genus varies considerably between species and hybrids, therefore the following information should only be read as a generalisation. When buying a 'Slipper Orchid' always try to make sure you know the exact species or hybrid type.

Paphiopedilums tend to prefer cooler conditions within the home and do not tolerate well temperatures above 30°C (86°F). Consequently conservatories should be avoided.

Shade is also a requirement, although access to light should be increased during the winter.

Paphiopedilums are terrestrial in the wild and should be planted in a less coarse, more water retentive medium than their epiphytic cousins.

Water these plants regularly allowing the compost to dry out a little between watering. Misting is only required on hot days and when the plant is growing strongly.

Slipper orchids can be susceptible to fungal disease. Take care when watering to avoid water collecting in the joints between leaf and shoots, as this can soon lead to rot.
Mealybug and scale insects are also fond of life in these joints.

Phalaenopsis

If you have just bought your first orchid, the odds are that it is a phalaenopsis. Over 75% of all orchid sales in the UK are of this type.

Commonly known as the 'Moth Orchid' (the white flowers in particular are said to resemble moths in flight). Phalaenopsis often flower for over six months of the year, require relatively low light levels and enjoy usual household temperatures.

The flat flowers are borne on gently arching stems. They are available in many colours and the flowers can be solid in colour, blotched or veined.

All phalaenopsis species are epiphytic in their natural habitat and produce an abundance of aerial roots.

They should be grown in a bark rich mixture but care should be taken not to let them dry out completely. Tepid water should be used when watering, as with most orchids over watering should be avoided. They benefit from misting (foliage only) which reflects the humidity of their tropical origin.

Although they prefer partial shade, some natural light is required to allow growth and flowering especially during the winter months.

In ideal conditions a temperature of 16° - 20°C (62 - 68°F) should be maintained throughout the year. Never let the temperature drop below 15°C (59°F).

After flowering cut the stem back to the second or third node. From this a new flowering stem should develop.

Mealybug and scale insect can be problematic, as can botrytis.

Phalaenopsis – 'Moth Orchid'

Oncidium

Sometimes known as 'Dancing Ladies', or in the USA, 'Butterfly Orchids'. Oncidium bear their ostentatious flowers in sprays along long stems. These sprays may be pruned back if they become too long.

Commonly the flowers are yellow in colour with brown stripes or spots.

Oncidiums also provide the added benefit of often being delightfully scented.

They are naturally epiphytic and should be grown in a medium to fine bark medium.

Oncidiums belong to a group of orchids known as the intergeneric hybrids.

The interbreeding and hybridisation that has taken place has resulted in many colours and forms being available. A further benefit is that complex maintenance requirements have been largely 'bred out' of the plants on sale in garden centres today.

Generally speaking Oncidium will thrive in similar light levels to those as required by phalaenopsis.

They are best kept in temperatures that do not exceed 29°C (85°F) during the day and do not fall below 15 – 18°C (60-65°F) at night.

Oncidiums, as with most other epiphytes will react badly to over watering as their roots are particularly vulnerable to rotting. Misting is recommended between waterings.

Like other epiphytes, oncidiums like to have good ventilation, however take care to avoid cold draughts.

Fungal diseases can be a problem. Good ventilation can help prevent these. Be wary for attack by mealybug and scale insect.

Oncidium

Zygopetalum

Zygopetalums are famed for their fragrance and star shaped flowers which are mostly spotted, marbled and usually last for several weeks.

They are native to the cool rain forests of South America, where they grow epiphytically.

Zygopetalum require more light than some other orchids, however they still need to be protected from strong summer sun.

Too much light will cause the leaves to turn yellowish in colour. Ideally the leaves need to be a mid – green colour.

A dark green leaf indicates that the plant is not receiving enough light and should be moved to a brighter location.

Although they originate from the relatively cooler rainforests they are quite adaptable to the temperature of their surroundings.

In summer they will thrive in temperatures between 12 - 30°C (55 – 86°F), however in the winter, the maximum temperature needs to be reduced to around 18°C (64°F).

Zygopetalum should not be allowed to dry out. The compost or growing medium should be kept moist at all times. Root rot is quite rare in this species but as with all orchids water logging must be avoided.

A special point of note with zygopetalum is that they prefer to be planted in large pots, this being a consequence of their proliferation of large roots.

Zygopetalum are prone to fungal disease, ensure good air movement around the plant and only mist sparingly. The usual suspects, mealybug, scale insect and red spider mite can cause a nuisance.

Feeding

Always use a good quality orchid feed such as 'Lorbex' specialist feeds.

Orchid Type	Feeding recommendations
Cattleya	Feed during spring and summer when new growth appears or every 2 – 3 weeks. Do not feed in winter months.
Cymbidium	A 'hungry' genus. Feed every other watering, or at ½ strength every watering. Feed throughout the year.
Dendrobium	Feed weekly when growing, and every other watering for the remainder of the year.
Miltonia	Miltonia have fragile roots. Feed during spring and summer with a ½ strength solution at every third watering.
Paphiopedilum	Recommendations vary according to exact species or hybrid. Feed every third watering if plant is growing.
Phalaenopsis	Feed throughout the year at every other watering. In winter feed at ½ strength.
Oncidium	Feed from the beginning of April until the end of October at every other watering. Feed every 5th watering in winter.
Zygopetalum	Feed every other watering throughout the year at full strength.

Pests & Diseases

Aphids

Easily recognisable as 'greenfly'. They tend to crowd together on the tips of new shoots, leaves and flowers. As well as sucking the sap they are also potential carriers of disease. For severe infestations treat with one of the many insecticides available at your local garden centre.

Mealybug

These are sap suckers which coat themselves in a white cotton wool like substance.
They particularly like hot conditions. On orchids they secrete themselves around pseudobulbs, underneath leaves and on stems. Their waxy coats help protect them from spray born insecticides. Small numbers can be easily removed from a plant by wiping with a damp cloth or cotton bud.

Larger numbers need to be treated with a systemic insecticide.
Repeat applications may be required according to manufacturers' instructions.

Red spider mite

Contrary to popular belief these microscopic pests are not visible to the naked eye. However they do produce characteristic 'webs' which can be seen. They are one of the most serious of orchid pests. They suck the plants sap resulting in a gradual yellowing of the leaves.
They thrive in hot, dry conditions. Frequent misting of the orchids foliage during the summer months is a good preventative measure. Orchid flowers should not be misted.

Scale Insects

These are visible as brown, slightly oval discs.

They are protected from spraying by their waxy shells. However like mealy bug, they can be removed by wiping with a damp cloth or cotton bud. After removal, spray the plant (avoiding any flowers) with an insecticide.

Whitefly

These are small white moth like insects. They are also sap suckers. Whitefly have a 'double whammy' effect. Firstly their feeding can really weaken the plant. Secondly, they produce a sticky substance called 'honeydew' which can encourage growth of black sooty mould.
Eradication is notoriously difficult especially if the plant is heavily infested. Treat with insecticide at regular intervals.

Whitefly can soon become resistant to certain chemicals. It is therefore recommended to alternate the type of insecticide used.

Diseases

These can be bacterial, fungal or viral.

Bacterial diseases often show as soft rots. They will occur if the plant is kept in overly wet conditions. They can spread very quickly and sometimes kill the plant in a few days. If the plant is not too badly infected it may be saved by cutting away the infected tissue and moving the plant to a drier location.

The most problematic *fungal* disease is botrytis. This affects cymbidium, cattleya, dendrobium and phalaenopsis in particular. Botrytis appears as a grey mould. Remove infected material, increase air movement and decrease humidity.

Viral diseases are difficult to diagnose. They usually cause abnormalities in the plant. Infected tissue should be destroyed. Make hygiene a priority.

NOTES